Light of the world, you
came into my darkness,
opened my eyes, and you
let me see.

Content

Staying in the Light
My mental health – my journey in faith

When I finished writing and getting my first book published, a little book called 'From Darkness to Light,' I never thought I would decide to write a second book. But here I am, writing the first couple of lines and wondering why I am doing this again!

I'm excited to share the personal journey I've been on in the second book, which revolves around staying true to the light that is Jesus. Keeping my life enlightened by the light Jesus has given me has transformed my way of thinking and looking at my life.

It's going to be a tough challenge, but I firmly believe that God will provide me with the strength and guidance I need to overcome it.

In this book, I will navigate back and forth through my journey with Jesus to illustrate how he has significantly supported me in various stages of our relationship.

Come along and explore the different chapters of this book, from the beginning of my special journey with Jesus, as well as the battles and other experiences that have kept me going and close to Jesus – baptism, worship, housegroup, creativity and most important of all for me prayer.

I'll also include a paragraph or two about the 'Armour of God,' which I believe is one of God's most blessed gifts.

I am not an expert in theology, a prophet, or a deeply educated Christian with an extensive knowledge of Bible scripture. However, the content of this book reflects my personal thoughts and experiences in my relationship with Jesus.

The Light
John 8:12

"I am the light of the world. Whoever follows me will never walk in darkness but will have the *light of life.*"

In the Bible, Jesus is referred to as light in the Gospel of John, where he claims to be the light of the world in John 8:12 and 9:5. The term "light" is used more than 30 times in the Gospel of John. In John 12:39, Jesus says, "I have come into the world as light, so that whoever believes in me may not remain in darkness".

Jesus also uses the phrase "light of the world" to describe himself and his disciples in the Gospel of Matthew (5:14–16). In this verse, Jesus explains that his disciples bring light to the world by following him, God, and the Holy Spirit.

When I refer to the light in the title of this book, I am referring to Jesus. He was the guiding light that came to me in my darkest moments, when I had reached a point of desperation. Without Jesus being there when I was at my lowest, I know I would not be here today. My gratitude and love for Jesus for saving my life are immense. He has given me a second chance, and I believe there is a purpose he has for me, which he will reveal as I continue to grow in my relationship and journey with him,

In my second book, my aim is to empower and guide others in deepening their connection with Jesus. The journey can take various forms such as engaging in meaningful conversations with a Christian, actively participating in church activities, enrolling in an Alpha Course for spiritual exploration, and finding solace and strength through prayer. These avenues offer diverse paths for individuals to seek and embrace their faith.

Before I continue, I want to admit that I struggle with reading the Bible. I usually listen to Bible scripture in a Bible app or through the 'The Bible with Nicky and Pippa Gumbel' App. This has helped me improve my knowledge of the word of God, and I see the Bible as my spiritual and daily guide.

Start of my journey.
Colossians 2:6-7

[6] And now, just as you accepted Christ Jesus as your Lord, you must continue to follow him. [7] Let your roots grow down into him, and let your lives be built on him. Then your faith will grow strong in the truth you were taught, and you will overflow with thankfulness.

The beginning of my journey/relationship with Jesus I've always believed, is the day he saved me from taking my own life. As I reflect on my almost 50 years of existence, I realize that this relationship goes back further to the day I was conceived and born into this world. But it wasn't until that day he saved me, that the true power of his love for me and how the light he would bring into my life has changed me as person.

When I was trying to work out how I could describe the love of Jesus to me, the following vison came to me:

when Jesus found me, he opened up my heart, he placed his heart inside and closed my heart around his, when my heart beats it is his blood that flows through my body with mine.

He has bound himself in me, in such a powerful way, that I can no longer be apart from him. Regardless of where life takes me and the trials, sorrows, joys, and laughter it brings, Jesus will always stand by me. His cleansing blood has the power to alleviate any pain or sorrow, while his unwavering love, which flows through every drop, sustains me during times of joy and love.

It is this connection that I have with Jesus which has kept me from ever going back to the darkness of suicide, and the grip of anxiety or depression caused by the abuse I suffered. Even when the anxiety creeps up, I know it won't last long, as Jesus dispels it from getting a grip.

Even today, it still amazes me how Jesus influences my daily life, especially on days when nothing seems to go right. I snap at my wife and daughter, frustration kicks in.. I usually bury my head in my phone for hours trying to deal with it, but as soon as I stop and say a prayer or just ask him for help, he brings everything into order, makes it possible to get things done and I am much more pleasant to live with.!

At the start of this chapter, I have quoted from the Bible, NLT version, Colossians chapter 2 verses 6 & 7, this is part of the apostle Paul's and Timothy's letter to the church in Colossae.

The letter is addressed to the people of Colossae. It serves as a reminder to follow

Jesus and use him as the foundation to build their lives upon. By doing so, they can grow their roots into Jesus, allowing their faith to grow stronger through the power of the truth that flows back up through those roots.

When I read through the words of these verses, I am reminded of the ongoing need to nurture and strengthen the foundations of my faith. The more open I am to the wisdom stemming from my roots, the more resilient my faith, love and appreciation for Jesus becomes

I truly believe it is essential for all Christians to hold onto these verses: we ought to continually express gratitude to Jesus for all he is doing in our lives, even when we are unaware of his presence. When we open our hearts to Jesus, he establishes an unbreakable bond with us, ensuring that he is constantly by our side.

As I reflect back on the start of this journey eight years ago, I had no idea where it would lead me or the depth of commitment I would develop to Jesus, and the reciprocated commitment he would have to me.

In the initial weeks after contemplating suicide, I took proactive steps to seek help and support from medical professionals and experts specializing in mental health. As part of this journey, I actively participated in a Cognitive Behavioural Therapy (CBT) course, which was designed to address and manage depression, anxiety, and related conditions. The course involved interactive sessions with a group of individuals, each grappling with varying levels of mental health challenges.

During one of the sessions, a form prompted us to disclose if we had experienced suicidal thoughts in the past two weeks, to which I admitted that I had been struggling with such thoughts. However, the experience of being in the group setting did not provide the level of support and understanding I had hoped for. Following the session, I was advised that the CBT course may not be the most effective approach for my specific needs.

Reflecting on this experience, it became clear to me that what I truly needed was the opportunity to engage in a one-on-one, in-depth conversation with someone who could actively listen and offer support without the constraints of medical protocol or group dynamics. I really was not sure where I was going to find this one-on-one place.

I do remember seeking help through multiple counselling sessions to address the impact of the physical and sexual abuse I endured during my teenage years, in the late 80's. These sessions provided me with a safe space to process my feelings and experiences, and I valued the support I received from my counsellors.

The expense was just too much for me at the time, so this really wasn't a feasible option for the suicide help I was looking for.

The only place where I found someone to listen to me about my abuse was at my church. I empathized with the lady I spoke to, and although she might not have fully understood what I was about to share, she kindly listened and let me talk about my experiences and how they affected my life.

The profound sense of relief that came with being able to open up and release the heavy burden of abuse that had weighed on my life at that time was immense. It brings to mind the saying, "A problem shared is a problem halved," and in this particular situation, the truth of that statement couldn't be more evident.

I realized that going to the church I was attending, was my best solution to finding what I was needing for my situation with the suicide and getting myself out of the mire I was in. This was not going to be an easy time, and I did pray for the strength and resilience to win this battle.

The Battles

Philippians 4:13
I can do all things through Christ who strengthens me.

In this chapter, I use the term "battle" to describe the intense struggle involved in maintaining one's mental, physical, and emotional well-being.

To me, it felt as though I was facing multiple battles simultaneously. These smaller battles had merged into one overwhelming conflict for me.

This collection of smaller battles can either stand alone or join forces to amplify their impact. Among these battles were fear and failure, which on their own are conquerable, but when they unite, it requires a deeper strength to combat them. Similarly, anxiety and depression were a pair of adversaries that, individually, could be overcome.

However, like fear and failure, together they presented a formidable challenge.

Furthermore, I grappled with sleep difficulties, resulting in constant fatigue and low energy levels. This made it difficult to focus on everyday tasks, and I found myself withdrawing from social interactions. Additionally, my unhealthy eating habits and decreased appetite became significant concerns.

these individual battles and multifaceted struggles ultimately took a heavy toll, as you will read, accumulated into a big full-on battle.

I lost all hope and allowed fear and failure to consume my thoughts. Nothing seemed to be going well. Balancing a job and providing for my family proved to be a constant struggle, and I found myself becoming increasingly difficult to be around.

Negative emotions took hold of me, draining away any sense of positivity or self-love, and also affecting my relationships with those closest to me. While some people are able to find solace in the good moments to combat the weight of the bad, I found it increasingly challenging as there were very few, if any, positive days for me to hold on to.

It was this overwhelming darkness and despair that consumed my mind, thoughts, and daily existence. I felt powerless to fight back or overcome the darkness, and nothing I tried seemed to work. At the time, I was still smoking 10-20 cigarettes a day, which initially helped to calm me in the mornings, but the relief didn't last long. While some people turn to drinking to cope, it wasn't an outlet for me, as I still held onto a fragment of sanity.

So, yes, the place I was in, was not a place I want to ever go back to.

As I wrapped up the last chapter, I made a firm decision to reach out for the help I needed, including professional and medical support, to start afresh and strive for a brighter future. In my heart, I knew that my church was the one place I could truly rely on.

In that moment, I felt a powerful sense of certainty that it was the presence of Jesus guiding and generously providing the support that I would soon come to rely on.

It's important to remind ourselves time and time again that Jesus understands us better than we understand ourselves. The immeasurable depth and vastness of his love is beyond our comprehension. His love knows no bounds and encompasses us in every possible way.

With the unwavering presence of Jesus in every aspect of my daily I found the courage to confront the formidable battles that loomed before me.

Even in the midst of these difficult battles, with Jesus by your side and deep within your heart, don't lose heart when all seems bleak and gloomy, because Jesus will give you the strength and you will succeed and overcome them.

One thing I should've mentioned before, but it's crucial to understand that the difficulties we encounter, such as fear and failure, do not stem from God. Instead, they are tools used by the evil one to obstruct your ability to embrace life fully and establish a deep, meaningful relationship with Jesus. These struggles are employed by the enemy as his sole method of impeding your spiritual journey.

Sometimes I think of these struggles as a bully lurking in the shadows, waiting to pounce on you. When you're feeling strong and clear-minded, you can spot him and push him back where he belongs. But when the darkness starts to creep in, you don't always see him coming, and he ends up getting the best of you.

I believe that my life is a testament to the overwhelming power and love of Jesus during challenging times. He has equipped me with the tools and protection to overcome any obstacles that try to take hold of me.

As with the previous chapters, I have quoted scripture from the Bible, one particular verse, Philippians 4:13, has consistently given me strength and guidance in numerous instances. I have even chosen to wear a cross bearing this powerful verse as a constant reminder of its significance in my life.

This verse serves as a poignant reminder that with Jesus's presence, we possess the ability to conquer even the most formidable challenges. It offers solace in the knowledge that, despite our struggles and stumbles, Jesus remains steadfast by our side, always ready to lift us up, brush us off, and set us back on the path forward.

I do remember I did get to speak with one of the elders at the church and I am still grateful to this day for their time and kindness at that time. Like the lady at my old church, they didn't judge or comment about it, they just listened.

Because of Jesus, I became more engaged with the youth church. Our daughter was still little at the time and was loving her time in kids' church, making friends, and learning about Jesus in a fun way, so it made sense to help out.

As well as spending precious time talking with others, as a way of fighting these battles, there has been other ways that have really helped keep ahead of these enemies. I will go into more detail in the next couple of chapters.

Worship – Singing and Praising Jesus

Psalm 100:2.
Worship the Lord with gladness; come before him with joyful songs

I also became involved in worship at the church. I've always had a passion for singing and started as a chorister at the age of 10. Whether I'm singing from the choir stalls or on stage, my goal remains the same – to praise and worship Jesus and bring the church community closer to him.

Being able to sing, praise and worship Jesus, has become fundamental in my rebuilding and growing of confidence in myself. It is also a great and powerful weapon against the small er battles.

Even if you lack confidence in your singing ability, it doesn't matter to Jesus. He understands that when you passionately express words of praise and joy for Him, whether it's in the solitude of your car or the privacy of your shower, or when you're wholeheartedly singing in church, you draw closer to Him. This connection is reinforced by the profound power of the spoken word, especially when it's rooted in scripture.

There is an abundance of incredibly moving and uplifting worship songs and hymns available for listening on platforms such as YouTube and Spotify. These songs have the power to provide a rejuvenating boost in the morning or at any time during the day. What makes them even more compelling is their foundation in scripture, with many old hymns directly quoting from the Bible. This provides an opportunity for individuals, including those who may not be avid readers, to immerse themselves in God's word through the act of listening to or singing worship music—an enriching and profound way to engage with scripture.

It is important to keep in mind that the devil despises worship. Whether we worship together or apart, whether we sing, praise, or pray, every syllable of God's word and every word of praise hurts and irritates him.

I assure you that the devil is a crafty individual who will employ every conceivable strategy to sidestep and evade God's truth. He will never give up on you, no matter how hard we attempt to stop him.

I mentioned the 'Armour of God' at the opening of this book, which consists of several pieces, each of which plays a role in our everyday life.

The 'Sword of the Spirit' depicts the Bible and the power of God's Word, which is why utilising scripture to worship, and praise is so effective in protecting us from the devil.

Gathering together to pray and worship is something I would encourage men, women, and children to do on a regular basis. Even simply listening to the worship - to allow Holy Spirit soaking, is a beautiful way to absorb Jesus into your heart, mind, body, and soul. Worshipping Jesus and inviting him into your every waking minute is the most incredible and life-changing thing you can do.

People receive such immense joy when we praise them with gladness and love, and I think this also happens to Jesus when we praise him.

When a church congregation sings and praises Jesus with all of their heart and soul, it is one of the most awesome sights to see. Some with their arms raised, reaching out for his embrace, and sometimes they even cry tears of pure happiness.

All I can say to anyone reading this book is when you are feeling down, sad and struggling to focus on anything – Put on some upbeat worship music and start singing until you feel the presence of the Holy Spirit. I often do this when driving the van at work or when I'm driving home. I do get strange glances, but it doesn't bother me because I'm filled with Jesus.

Now if you are at home, you can sing and dance, and if you are fortunate, you can bless your neighbours with worship!

So, as I conclude this chapter, I have curiously been listening to worship songs while writing and typing. It absolutely helps with connecting with God, working with him on the words to type, and checking to see if what I'm writing works and if he's happy... and when I go on, I know everything is OK.

Baptism of water & fire!
John 3:5:
"In Baptism, we are "born of water and the Spirit".

In July 2018, I felt a strong desire to deepen my relationship with Jesus. After much reflection and prayer, I decided to get baptized again. Although I was baptized as a baby, this time I chose to have a full submersion baptism. Fortunately, our church had a baptism pool built under the auditorium floor. After several meetings with the church pastor, everything was set for my baptism, or as we joked, being "dunked"!

in November 2018, I along with 3 others, took our place by the pool and in front of the church congregation and shared our testimonies of why we were being baptised. It was a particularly vulnerable moment for me as it marked the first time I had openly discussed my struggle with suicidal thoughts in front of such a large group of people. I vividly remember feeling exposed and apprehensive about their potential judgment. However, their reaction was different than I expected. Some individuals provided me with thoughtful words of encouragement and shared meaningful scriptures, while others were visibly moved by my testimony. Witnessing the genuine care and compassion deeply touched my heart and affirmed the supportive nature of the congregation.

I was certainly unsure of how I would feel being baptised, even with all the preparation beforehand, you just don't quite know what will happen to you, apart from being soaked.

I was second in line to be baptised, and I had asked a close friend from the church to assist the pastor in dunking me, knowing he would be able to lift me back out again!

When we entered the pool, the water was still cold, but this was not a big problem, as it will be quick. The pastor asked a few questions, the whole church was stood around watching and then I was baptised.

When I was lifted back out of the water, everything seemed clearer and brighter. My feelings were undoubtedly different. It felt as if I had been utterly scrubbed clean on the inside; I believed and felt like I was a new person, not of this world but of God.

If your relationship with Jesus is just getting started, I would strongly advise you to speak with your church or a local church about getting baptised—or getting baptised again if you were previously christened as a baby or toddler. It is undoubtedly among the greatest methods, in my opinion, to draw nearer to Jesus.

Of course, allowing Jesus into your life is the first and most important step, but in my opinion, this is one of the biggest commitments you can make to Him.

The title of this chapter relates to baptism by water and fire, and you may be wondering how you can be baptised by fire. However, this fire is the fire of the Holy Spirit.

I won't attempt to cover every detail of the Holy Spirit's baptism because there is a wealth of information available in literature and on the internet. I'll just talk about how I experienced the baptism of the Holy Spirit and how he has affected me personally.

When do I believe I received my baptism of the Holy Spirit? That is a difficult question to answer; if I think back not just to the past eight years, but beyond, there are many times when I could say, "That is when it happened," but for me, the first time I truly experienced and realised that the Holy Spirit was a part of me was when I attended a 'Alpha Course' Holy Spirit away day. I will tell you more about the Alpha Course in a later chapter.

the overwhelming sensation of my entire body being filled with a soothing warmth, rather than a burning heat, was something I had never felt before.

Initially, I thought I was imagining this, and it was the awkward feeling you get when you're in a crowd of people, but no - others in the group, I noticed, were experiencing similar feelings and some had tingling in their hands, while others had nothing.

So, if they were having similar experiences at the same time, and the group's leaders acknowledged this, I knew I was being filled and baptised by the Holy Spirit.

That experience was incredibly moving and made me feel as though I had received some type of "superpower." It was comparable to my water baptism in that it brought me clarity and purification in both my heart and mind.

Since that moment, I have come to know when the Holy Spirit is working with in me. As well as the warmth inside, both my hands heat up and other times I am restless on my feet.

A few months after I attended the Alpha Course, just when the COVID lockdowns began, my mother-in-law was very ill in hospital. When we had gone to see her, I had been waiting outside the hospital and felt the need to pray.

So, I did; I prayed for her health and for the family, and then I received a call to come up and see her. When we got to her she really wasn't well at all, and I felt compelled to pray again. At the time, I wasn't the best at prayer, generally in my head with the occasional grumble. But, without thinking, I extended my hands in front of me, towards my mother-in-law, and prayed for healing, asking God to fill her with life, and repeated it several times. I did get some weird looks from other patients on the ward, but it didn't matter.

We discovered not long after we left her that she had sat up in bed and was alive - it was absolutely a miracle, and even the doctor couldn't quite comprehend how she was still alive - but thank God she was.

I understood then that it was the Holy Spirit who had prompted me to pray and given me the words to say. If I hadn't attended the Alpha Course when I did, I doubt I would have prayed, and who knows what would have happened.!

I now understand how profoundly privileged I am to Have received the gift of the Holy Spirit from Jesus.

Because I choose to follow and accept Jesus as my Lord and Saviour, I am now baptised with not only holy water but also the fire of the Holy Spirit.

It is up to the other people to tell you how they personally encounter the Holy Spirit, but you can tell by looking at them, by the way they speak, and by their faces that the Spirit of God is at work in their lives.

Housegroup – an extended Christian family

Acts 1:14

They all joined together constantly in prayer, along with the women and Mary the mother of Jesus, and with his brothers.

~

Matthew 18:20

For where two or three gather in my name, there am I with them

But one place I found has become a wee gem of help, was our church housegroup.

So, what is a housegroup? A housegroup, sometimes known as a homegroup or home-church, is a group of Christians that meet on a regular basis in private homes for worship, bible study, prayer, and exploring aspects of their Christian faith and of course, catching up on each other's news.

I sometimes believe that these homegroups serve as a strong backbone for each church that has them; they keep members of the congregation feeling valued and known, and they keep those on the edges informed of what is going on and aware that they are loved.

The earliest 'housegroup' is described in the book of Acts 1:13—when Jesus met with his followers in the 'upper room'—and in verse 14, they congregate regularly in prayer, along with the women, Jesus' Mother Mary, and his brothers.

So homegroups are not a new thing, and many homegroups over the years have grown into new churches.

Following my wife, I joined the housegroup at my current church, which has been a true blessing for us both. Even though everyone there was at a different point in their Christian journey, we were all learning something new about God's word. The group was mostly made up of couples, and we all got along great and went to social events together.

I have without a doubt, learnt a huge amount from this housegroup about how faith, prayer, a better understanding of scripture, and coming together as Christians has helped to make me a better Christian. Not just for myself, but for my family as well.

I was inspired to pray more and to pray out loud by our housegroup. I saw this as a challenge to be a more courageous and to have faith in the things I was praying for, rather than as a critique of the prayers I was saying.

As they say, "all good things must come to an end," and regrettably, the group disbanded after around four years. God was calling several couples to do different things. One pair is currently running their own housegroup and the church's Alpha Course, while another couple works from home doing similar things. These amazing individuals are a blessing to the church and shining examples of their Christian faith.

My wife and I sensed a calling from God that went in a somewhat different route than the others, and we believed he was telling us to continue praying. After a few months of discussion, we organised our own homegroup, with an emphasis on intercessional prayer and using worship to get closer to God in our prayers.

If there is one blessing and piece of advice I could give you, the reader, it is to look for homegroups at the church you feel comfortable and at home in. I am sure you can test each one out to see which one works best for you and then get involved.

Faith in Prayer
Mark 11:24

"Therefore, I tell you, whatever you ask for in prayer, believe that you have received it, and it will be yours"

Prayer has been the one thing I have learnt to rely on above everything else. Praying for God to forgive me of my sins, for my family, and for anything else that comes to mind that needs prayer has become a regular part of my morning commute to work.

The one thing I have to remind myself of is to continue to have trust in my prayers and to ask for God's blessing on them - and as long as I have faith, those blessings and prayers will come through.

When I was younger and in my teens, I didn't pray that much since it wasn't something I felt comfortable doing openly or in my head. I always struggled to find the perfect words and would stutter and stumble over what I was trying to convey. Let's say I had little faith in what I was doing. Yes, I attended church and Sunday school, but as previously stated in this book, I did not have a strong and meaningful relationship with God.

Therefore, I had little desire to spend time praying, reading the Bible, or doing anything similar. Playing football with my friends or using my PlayStation made me happier.

It wasn't until I got married that I decided to give praying another chance. I still didn't pray aloud because it wasn't something we did at church when I was younger, and the prayers in my brain often sounded far better than when I spoke them out loud.

When I think about it now, the reason the words sounded so great in my head was because God put them there, he had arranged the words perfectly, so had I the confidence and belief myself and him, when prayed it out loud it would be great.!

But I lacked confidence in myself back then; I had low self-esteem and battled to be optimistic about everything. I still have periods of self-doubt, but I know that with prayer and faith in those prayers, everything will be well.

What then am I attempting to impart to you regarding prayer and praying? Well, I would like to urge you to begin praying and not to be ashamed of it. You are essentially speaking with God and no one else.

Praying for me is about developing a personal relationship with Jesus and God, and as part of that relationship, you can bring your cares and fears, whether they are about yourself or about family members.

Even when your mind is racing and you have a lot to juggle and organise, all I can advise is to offer it to Jesus in prayer.

In the bible, Matthew 11:28-30 says the following:

Come to me, all you who are weary and burdened, and I will give you rest. [29] Take my yoke upon you and learn from me, for I am gentle and humble in heart, and you will find rest for your souls. [30] For my yoke is easy and my burden is light."

Jesus desires to take on and release your troubles. He then extends his easy yoke and light loads to you, allowing us to directly learn from him how to handle our difficulties. However, in order to be set free, you must first pray to him.

But as a Christian, probably the most used and import prayer to me, is the one Jesus taught us, the 'Lord's Prayer.'

The Lord's Prayer is a daily reminder that can help people live well and flourish in many ways:

- Acknowledges imperfections

The prayer acknowledges that people fall short and need to forgive others.

- Reminded of a constant need for forgiveness

The prayer is a reminder of the constant need for forgiveness, which can be difficult to hear.

- Be resilient in a challenging world

The prayer reminds people that life is difficult, but that strength and help are available in God.

- Understand the end of the story

The prayer reminds people that God holds the end of the story, and that God will bring all things to completion.

So, I will bring this chapter to a close with
the words of the Lord's Prayer.:

Our Father in heaven,
hallowed be your name,
your kingdom come,
your will be done,
on earth as in heaven.
Give us today our daily bread.
Forgive us our sins
as we forgive those who sin against
us.
Lead us not into temptation
but deliver us from evil.
For the kingdom, the power,
and the glory are yours
now and for ever.
Amen

Repentance

1 John 1:9

If we confess our sins, he is faithful and just and will forgive us our sins and purify us from all unrighteousness.

I was unsure whether to include anything about repentance when I was praying over what I wanted to write about in this book, and what aspects of my journey with Jesus I felt would be helpful to others. However, the more I thought about it, the more I realised how crucial it is for us to continue in our relationship with Jesus by confessing our sins and turning from them.

The Lord's Prayer makes this quite clear: "And forgive us our sins, as we forgive those who sin against us." As a result, there is actually no justification for not repenting.

As a Christian, it is unquestionably crucial to approach Jesus in prayer, confess our faults, and ask for forgiveness of those sins. This helps to create a closer relationship with him and a clearer, purer heart and mind.

We must not only confess our own sins but also ask for the pardon of those who have wronged us. This is really important, in my opinion, because if we are asking God to forgive us of our own faults, then we also need to be willing to forgive others.

I am aware that some Christians believe that since Jesus died on the cross to atone for all of our sins, repentance is unnecessary. However, I believe it doesn't mean we are exempt from sin—after all, we are fallible human beings who make mistakes both towards God and other people. Therefore, we must ask for forgiveness and turn from our sins in order to make amends.

How does repentance help me on my journey with Jesus and with my mental health issues? For me, praying for forgiveness for any sins I have committed, both deliberately and unknowingly, against God and others has been part of my daily prayer to God.

Now, after thanking God for a fresh day in my morning prayers, I occasionally forget to ask for repentance. But I make sure to include it before I finish, because I'm sure he discreetly reminds me!

I know that by repenting, as well as asking for God's blessings of wisdom, knowledge, discernment, and a better understanding of these sins, I will be relieved of the anxiety and stress that these sins will cause.

Without question, prayer has become a requirement for me. It is an essential part of my faith and relationship with Jesus that I cannot function without.

Since I firmly believe that Jesus hears my prayers, forgives my sins, and accepts my true repentance, I am confident that I begin each day with a clear conscience and a positive outlook.

So, my suggestion to you, the reader, is to give prayer a try; it will not hurt you, and if your heart is in those prayers, I know God is with you, hearing you, and blessing you.

Armour of God

Ephesians 6:13
Therefore, put on the full armour of God, so that when the day of evil comes, you may be able to stand your ground, and after you have done everything, to stand

"The Armour of God" links the elements of Christianity to the gear used by Roman soldiers. The armour consists of:

Belt of truth: Protects against lies from the enemy

Breastplate of righteousness: A piece of the armour of God protects our hearts

Shoes of the gospel of peace: A piece of the armour of God they allow us to walk without fear.

Shield of faith: Shields against attacks from the devil

Helmet of salvation: Protects the mind from doubt cast by the devil

Sword of the Spirit: The word of God, which is the only offensive weapon in the armour

The apostle Paul instructs the Ephesians to put on the "armour of god" in order to thwart the devil's plans in Ephesians 6:10–17. He also describes each piece and how to use it.

As a young Christian growing up into my teens and twenties, I had never heard of God's armour, and I had no idea it existed.

Even after being married and becoming more involved in church, the armour held little importance for me, let alone its purpose.

It wasn't until our housegroup decided to hold a couple of meetings about the 'Armour of God' and how each component plays a role in our daily and Christian lives, that I realised how important it would be for me, especially with my mental health.

I am forever grateful for those meetings and for the shared knowledge of those leading.

These days, I make sure to put on my armour spiritually and mentally before I leave the house. God protects my wife & my daughters in their day because I pray, they are wearing their armour as well.

I chose Ephesians 6:13 to begin this chapter because it serves as a daily reminder to me that the devil is constantly planning and prowling; he never sleeps, so as long as I wear my armour and pray and repent, the devil has very little power over me.

It can, of course, take a beating, just like any other armour, and chinks may form if the damaged pieces are not replaced or repaired. The devil can enter via these chinks, which is why I personally get anxious and occasionally grumpy. I usually locate a quiet area and pray and tell the demon to clear off.!

So, ensuring that you obtain fresh armour on a regular basis would undoubtedly help with the mental conflicts that the devil will throw at you.

I'm not sure how this applies to other Christians, but I can tell that I'm becoming better at keeping my shield in place and using my sword more effectively. The more I learn about the Bible and how many passages and chapters I can use to defend myself against attacks, the more comfortable and user-friendly the armour gets.

My advice, if you wish to take it, is to read Ephesians 6:10–17 and see how you can use your armour in your battles and daily challenges. With so much madness in this world – ongoing conflicts, pandemics, and corruption – basically just anything that is evil, we as Christians, with our armour on and with God and his angels beside us, can take on this evilness and conquer it all. This image is a great visual of how the armour of God, the apostle Paul was describing:

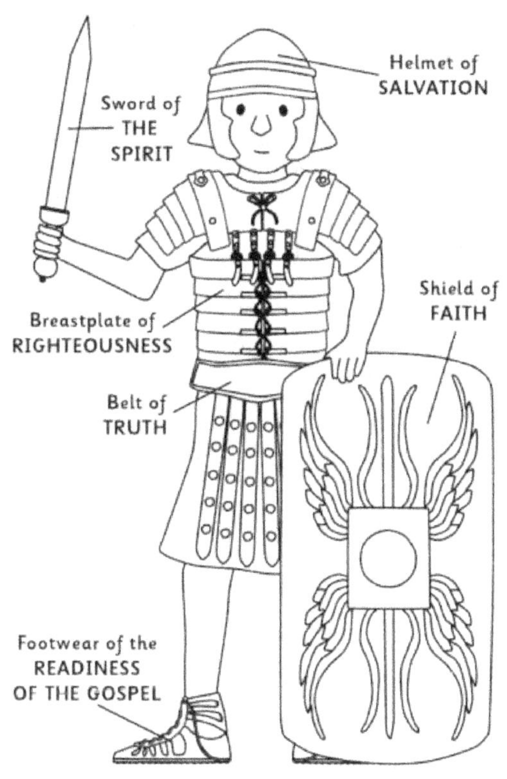

Reading the Bible is something I do struggle with, as I indicated way back at the beginning of this book, even though I know as a Christian I should be making more of an effort to do this. However, I have managed to get my head inside the Bible in different ways. I've discovered that listening to narrated versions of Bible books helps me better understand what is written. I've downloaded podcasts that do just that.

Additionally, I downloaded the Bible as an app to my phone, which has been a really helpful method to access verses for a variety of purposes. Without a doubt, I would advise downloading this app!

Along with many other Christians, I have come upon 'Bible in a Year,' a project by Nicky & Pippa Gumble. I listen to this on a daily basis now, especially on my commute to work.

In the following chapter, I'll go into more detail about this and other fascinating ways to learn more about Jesus.

The Alpha Course & The Bible with Nicky and Pippa Gumbel App

Matthew 11:29
Take my yoke upon you and learn from me, for I am gentle and humble in heart, and you will find rest for your souls.

Alpha International has given me permission to reference them in this chapter, and I am very grateful for this.

When I started writing this book and deciding what to include in it, I wanted to make sure that it would be beneficial and have God's blessing. I felt compelled to add a chapter about the Alpha Course and 'The Bible with Nicky and Pippa Gumbel' app because both have profoundly grounded me and provided structure in my daily life.

I will share firstly about the Alpha Course:

The Alpha course is an evangelistic program designed to introduce the fundamentals of the Christian faith through a series of talks and discussions. It is described as "an opportunity to explore the meaning of life."

Alpha courses are conducted in churches, homes, workplaces, prisons, universities, and other locations.

It involves a series of sessions over 10 weeks, which includes a day away. Each session begins with a meal, followed by a video, talk, and discussions in small groups.

In my opinion, Alpha has become a foundational part of the Christian faith, not only in the UK but in any country where churches have adopted it. The success and popularity of Alpha can be attributed to Nicky Gumbel, who took over the leadership of the course in 1990.

I have had the privilege of attending two Alpha courses, one on my own and the second with my wife, both at my current church.

Even though we covered the same videos and had discussions in both courses, the overall effect it has had on me personally and on us as a couple has been amazing.

Unfortunately, due to Covid, the course was never completed because of the lockdowns. However, we were fortunate to have the opportunity to participate in the Holy Spirit Day retreat. It was one of the first times I had experienced the presence of the Holy Spirit within and around me. That session completely changed me for the better.

In an earlier chapter, *'Baptism of water & fire'*, I shared how the Spirit away day had empowered me to pray for my mother-in-law in hospital, where the Doctors had given her no hope of surviving, but he power of prayer and faith in those prayers kept her alive and I believe, the opportunity to fulfil the will God had placed on her heart.

If I hadn't attended the Alpha Course, I'm certain I wouldn't have prayed that day. I would have disregarded the urge to pray. I realised then that I really needed to attend the course again and this time complete it.

It was a good three to four years until attending an Alpha Course again, this time, I managed to persuade my wife to attend with me. Interestingly, she had participated in the course back in the 90s.
I strongly believe that this particular course provided us with a wonderful opportunity to come together and openly share our personal faith journeys and experiences with the other participants. It was a truly blessed and memorable time for all of us.

For those who are embarking on a new chapter in their Christian journey or seeking to invigorate their spiritual connection, the

Alpha course is an excellent opportunity to delve deeper into the impact of Jesus in our daily lives. I wholeheartedly encourage you to consider enrolling in an Alpha course at a nearby church.

I'd like to tell you about the " The Bible with Nicky and Pippa Gumbel" app, which my wife introduced me to. She had been using it for several months, and initially, I was unsure about how much I would use it. However, I eventually gave it a try and I'm really glad I did!

Every morning, I make sure to listen to the app without fail, most of the time during my commute to work. I personally prefer the express version, as I find the normal version too long for my drive. I also like to fit my prayers in before work!

I will admit that I have occasionally missed one or two, but I do find time to catch up with them, either while walking the dog or during a moment I get to myself.

Listening to the Bible scriptures, both old and new testaments, and hearing from individuals like Nicky Gumbel and his wife Pippa, who share their knowledge and understanding of the Bible and their personal experiences, makes using the app a relatable and easy-to-understand experience.

All I can do is recommend getting the 'The Bible with Nicky and Pippa Gumbel' app and giving it a try. I do think you will be pleasantly surprised by how much you will gain from it!

Other Adventures to try.!
Joshua 1:9
Have I not commanded you? Be strong and courageous. Do not be afraid; do not be discouraged, for the Lord your God will be with you wherever you go."

Having previously mentioned the Alpha course, there are numerous other Christian church-based adventures, festivals, and retreats that will all inspire your passion for Jesus!

In the UK, there have been a number of highly successful and spiritually uplifting gatherings, such as *'New Wine'*, *'Big Church Festival'*, *'CreationFest'*, *'David's Tent'*, *'New Horizons'*, and many others.

It's worth noting that Christian festivals are not limited to the UK and are held all around the world. While many churches attend these festivals as groups, individuals are also welcome to participate and experience the uplifting and enriching environment.

I have had the pleasure and joy of being a part of a Christian group called "The Filling Station." I've been able to lead worship, attend local meetings, and even go to one of their conferences. Being part of this group has allowed me to engage in more healing prayers and improve my prayer life. It's been amazing to witness the Holy Spirit's power and blessings during our meetings.

I would definitely recommend talking to your church about the events they attend or even organise themselves. My church regularly attends the 'New Wine' festival, where they camp together as a group and participate in worship and other activities. At one of my previous churches, they organized a community day for local residents every year, during which the church was open with a variety of stalls and entertainment.

If you're the adventurous type and prefer to explore on your own, take a thorough look online to find out about events in your area. There are so many options to choose from, so I'm sure you'll find the right one for you.

Being Creative – Drawing & Painting

Ephesians 2:10
For we are God's handiwork, created in Christ Jesus to do good works, which God prepared in advance for us to do

As I reflect on the incredible talents of renowned artists such as Michelangelo, Turner, and Van Gogh, I am filled with awe at the beauty and depth of their artwork. Their unique creativity and ability to produce such remarkable masterpieces bring immense joy and inspiration to all who admire their work.

The ultimate source of creativity, in my opinion, is God. He is the creator of everything we perceive: the vast heavens and the earth, the diverse animals and creatures, the lush trees, plants, and flowers, the breathtaking countryside, and most importantly, He created each and every one of us.

Being creative has become one of my ways of maintaining a positive mindset and warding off negative thoughts and struggles. I believe I have been blessed with the ability to draw, and I have created many sketches over the years. I am thankful to God for giving me this gift as an outlet for my challenges

Over the past few years, I've discovered a passion for creating and painting crosses. It brings me immense joy to see my crosses adorning the walls of people's homes, knowing that they are bringing comfort and happiness to those living there. Additionally, I'm proud to have my large painted crosses displayed in two local churches, where I hope they serve as symbols of God's love and peace for all who encounter them.

Painting and drawing are not the only sources of creativity. Many of you may have other ways to ignite your imagination in a creative manner. I know some people who are passionate about gardening, while others have created banners for our church. So, whatever you choose to do, give it a try and see what brings you joy and strengthens your relationship with Jesus.

(Sample of one of my crosses)

What Next..?

Hebrews 11:1

Now faith is the substance of things hoped for, the evidence of things not seen.

So, what now? I have shared what I have done so far in how my journey with Jesus has grown and, in some way, blossomed into a wonderful and joyful adventure and relationship. Of course, as mentioned, the journey isn't perfect, and I have slipped from the path numerous times. However, because Jesus is well and truly a part of my life and beside me on this journey, he helps me up and gets me back on track.

I cannot fully express the immense gratitude and love I have for Jesus. The change he has brought to my life is immeasurable.

The positive impact this has had on my relationship with my family has been wonderful.

I know that as I get older, I am more prone to grumpiness or becoming engrossed in my mobile phone and only half listening, which I know can be frustrating for those close to me, but I also know that I am a damn right better human being than the one who didn't want to be alive, and I can only attribute this to Jesus; no ifs and buts, he is the real deal, and I couldn't be without him in my life.

When choosing a Bible verse to begin this chapter, one of my favourites, and one I like to remind people of, is Hebrews 11:1

Maintaining your faith in everything that Jesus is doing in your life is the one thing I have learnt to rely on above all else.
He is aware of what is in store for us, even when we are unable to see it or accept it,

and he will make every effort to make it known to us as soon as the time is right, and we require it. Because he knows us better than we do—he is aware of our strengths and weaknesses, as well as whether or not we can withstand certain stresses.

If you have not yet begun to explore or investigate who Jesus is and how he might be a part of your life, I strongly encourage you to do so; you will not be disappointed.

Look for a church where you feel at home. If you're not ready to commit to a church, discover if there's a Christian organisation or charity in your area that can support and mentor you.

By striking up a conversation with someone at the church, Christian organisation, or charity, you will start to notice how much Jesus shines through in their interactions with you. This may truly help you feel at ease and confirm that you are in the right place.

Through this book, you may have observed that prayer is the one thing I do most of and is unquestionably a proven and tested technique to begin your relationship and journey with Jesus. I can assure you that it does the trick.!

So, this is the final paragraph in this book, I can guarantee you that I couldn't have anticipated writing more than double the pages of my first book, and I can only put this down to the encouragement and support of my family, but also that I have Jesus by me when I write.

Amen.

Final prayer

Dear Lord,

I pray to you with all my heart and soul, thanking you for everything you have done for me throughout my life. From the day I was born, to my darkness and being the light that saved me.

I pray you are the light in the darkness of others, guiding them to a safe place and on their path with you. I pray that you would pick them up when they stumble, as you have for me, and hug them in times of peace and rest.

With your love and blessing, I bring this prayer to you, in the name of my Saviour Jesus,

Amen

Useful Links

Alpha Course:
Either speak with a church rep or visit
https://alpha.org/

The Bible with Nicky and Pippa Gumbel App
Can be downloaded from Google Play store or Apple's App Store. Or visit their website -
https://bible.alpha.org/en/

The Filling Station:
Visit **https://thefillingstation.org/find-a-station/** for more information and location of your local venue.

'New Wine'
Visit **https://www.new-wine.org/** for more information on what they do and future events.

'Big Church Festival'
Visit **https://www.bigchurchfestival.com/** for more information on what they do and future events.

'CreationFest'
Visit **https://creationfest.org.uk/** for more information on what they do and future events.

'David's Tent',
Visit **https://www.davidstent.net/** for more information on what they do and future events.

'New Horizons'
Visit **https://newhorizon.org.uk/** for more information on what they do and future events.

Jesus,

It is you who lights up this world
before us.

Without your light, we would be in
continuous darkness, never knowing
the beauty you have made.
I pray you will return soon to
cleanse this earth of all darkness
and provide hope and joy to
everyone